Jam Pot

by Giulia Verzariu
illustrated by Steve Henry

Decodable 8

McGraw Hill Education

Bothell, WA • Chicago, IL • Columbus, OH • New York, NY

MHEonline.com

Send all inquiries to:
McGraw-Hill Education
8787 Orion Place
Columbus, OH 43240

ISBN: 978-0-02-145471-6
MHID: 0-02-145471-X

Printed in China

9 10 11 12 13 DSS 28 27 26 25 24

Jim, a big jam pot!

Jim, grab the jam pot!

Jim flips for fig jam!

See Fran jog in fog.

See the jam pot drop.

Fran drops jam for Jim!